Gold in the American River

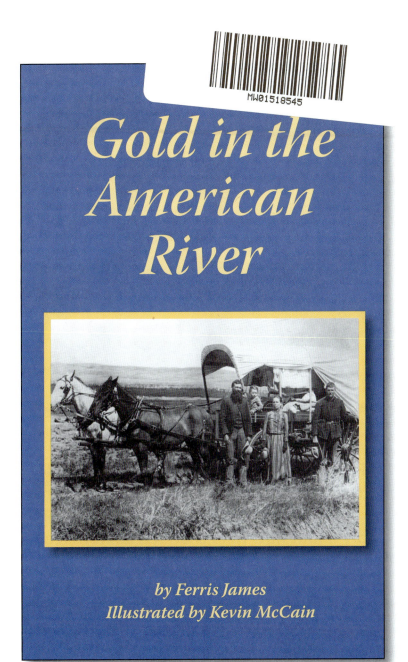

by Ferris James
Illustrated by Kevin McCain

Glenview, Illinois • Boston, Massachusetts • Chandler, Arizona
Upper Saddle River, New Jersey

Did you ever look at rings or necklaces made of gold? Did you ever wonder where the gold came from? This is the story of gold in California. This is the story about how gold changed California and America forever.

In the 1830s, a man named John Sutter left his home in a country called Switzerland and went to California. He wanted to start a huge ranch, or farm. He bought cattle. He hired workers. He thought his dream would come true.

---

cattle: cows, bulls, and steers

"Gold in the American River!"

James Marshall worked on Mr. Sutter's ranch. Mr. Marshall was building a sawmill. A sawmill is a place where logs from trees can be cut into lumber. In those times, sawmills were powered by water. This one was being built on the American River

On January 24, 1848, Mr. Marshall was standing by the river. Suddenly he saw something shiny and yellow. Mr. Marshall put his hand into the water. There was a piece of gold! He looked again. Gold was all around this place!

---

lumber: wood cut and prepared to use in buildings

James Marshall hurried back to see John Sutter. He told John Sutter all about the gold. Mr. Sutter was not interested. He did not want people coming onto his ranch to look for gold.

Mr. Sutter told Mr. Marshall not to tell anyone about the gold that he had found. But Mr. Sutter's workers had seen the shiny gold among the sand and rocks in the American River. They could not keep the gold a secret!

In the nearby city of San Francisco, Sam Brannan heard about the gold on John Sutter's land. He asked to see it. Sam Brannan became very excited. He took a bottle of gold dust and ran through the streets of San Francisco shouting, "Gold! Gold in the American River!"

Men and women came running to see the shiny yellow gold in the bottle. They were excited. People ran to buy shovels. They rushed to the American River. They all wanted gold! This was the beginning of the California Gold Rush.

The Gold Rush

During 1848 and 1849, news about the gold spread. Many people wanted to go to California. But in 1849, <mark>transportation</mark> was a big problem. There were no roads, no cars, no planes, and no train tracks to California. People could get there only by ship or by covered wagon.

Ships had to travel all the way around South America. They had to sail south on the Atlantic Ocean and then north on the Pacific Ocean. This trip took almost a year. Some ships ran out of drinking water and food. Other ships sank. Many people died.

---

transportation: ways of moving people and things from one place to another

Traveling to California on land was also very hard. People in covered wagons had to cross thousands of miles of wild country. Animals had to pull heavy wagons across rivers and over mountains. The trip across America took many months. Animals died. People died. Many who had left their families to look for gold never came back.

People from many lands all over the world joined the California Gold Rush.

Reaching California

Many thousands of people went to California looking for gold. They had caught *gold fever,* the great desire to find gold. They came from all over the world. They came from all over the United States. They came in boats and wagons. Everyone rushed to California with a dream of getting rich.

When the travelers arrived, many overran John Sutter's ranch. They trampled his corn and wheat fields. They killed his cattle for food. They broke down his house and used the wood. They built camps and towns all along the American River.

---

trampled: crushed, destroyed

Impact of the Gold Rush

Pollution and Destruction: In the beginning, gold was easy to find. But soon miners had to spend hours and hours each day in cold water, trying to find gold. Some miners got together and formed companies. Companies bought machines to get the gold out of the ground faster. The machines caused floods and pollution. They ruined some clean rivers in California.

Native Americans: Native American lands were overrun by gold miners as well. It did not matter who lived on the land first. If miners were looking for gold, they did not want Native Americans in their way. The way of life of many Native Americans was destroyed.

Extend Language **Expressions Using Gold**

In English there are many expressions that use the words *gold* or *golden*.

Gold fever: great desire to look for gold

Golden State: a name for the state of California

Good as gold: very good, excellent

Golden anniversary: fifty-year anniversary

Gold medal: first place in a sports competition

---

way of life: customs and traditions

Cooperation: Chinese, Europeans, Mexicans, and Americans all went to California to look for gold. People worked side by side. Some of them helped each other. People from many countries worked together. They learned about new cultures. They learned to accept one another.

Economics and Business: Many people in California made money selling food, water, clothes, and tools to the gold miners. A man named Levi Strauss made strong heavy pants for the gold miners. These pants were "blue jeans." Blue jeans are still popular today.

Another man named Phillip Armour sold meat to the gold miners. He opened a factory that put meat in cans. His factory is still working today.

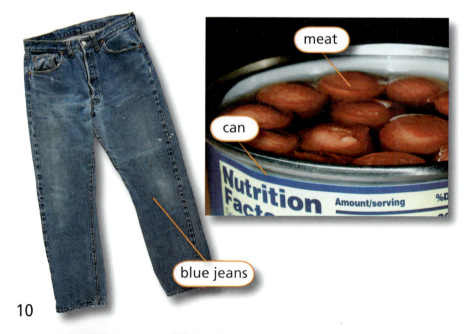

blue jeans

meat

can

The Gold Rush Spirit Lives On

The California Gold Rush ended when it became too difficult to find gold. Towns became vacant, or empty. People moved away. But California was changed forever. Many people with a spirit of adventure stayed in California. They found other jobs or opened new businesses. People from many places learned to accept each other. They learned about different foods, customs, and cultures. They continued to work hard.

The Gold Rush ended in California more than 100 years ago. But California is still a place where people from many cultures live and work. San Francisco is still a big city where people come to make a new life for themselves.